IT'S A SNAP!

GEORGE EASTMAN'S FIRST PHOTOGRAPH

Monica Kulling   *Illustrated by Bill Slavin*

TUNDRA BOOKS

For Nancy,
picture-perfect partner and friend
M.K.

For Ted,
the entrepreneur in our family
B.S.

Text copyright © 2009 by Monica Kulling
Illustrations copyright © 2009 by Bill Slavin

Published in Canada by Tundra Books,
75 Sherbourne Street, Toronto, Ontario M5A 2P9

Published in the United States by Tundra Books of Northern New York,
P.O. Box 1030, Plattsburgh, New York 12901

Library of Congress Control Number: 2008910107

Library and Archives Canada Cataloguing in Publication

Kulling, Monica, 1952-
   It's a snap! : George Eastman's first photograph / Monica Kulling ; Bill Slavin, illustrator.

ISBN 978-0-88776-881-1

1. Eastman, George, 1854-1932 – Juvenile literature. 2. Kodak camera – Juvenile literature. 3. Photographic industry – United States – Biography – Juvenile literature. 4. Inventors – United States – Biography – Juvenile literature. I. Slavin, Bill II. Title.

TR140.E3K84 2009   j770.92   C2008-907125-5

We acknowledge the financial support of the Government of Canada through the Book Publishing Industry Development Program (BPIDP) and that of the Government of Ontario through the Ontario Media Development Corporation's Ontario Book Initiative. We further acknowledge the support of the Canada Council for the Arts and the Ontario Arts Council for our publishing program.

ONTARIO ARTS COUNCIL
CONSEIL DES ARTS DE L'ONTARIO

Medium: Pen and ink with watercolor on paper
Design: Leah Springate

Printed in Canada

1 2 3 4 5 6   14 13 12 11 10 09

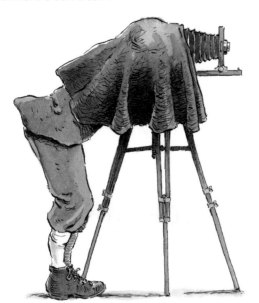

Making History

Today is a holiday.
I hold a camera
and frame your face,
whenever you look my way.

I line up light
to make you shine.
I line you up
to make you mine.

Move forward. Move left.
Move back. Move right.
Give yourself
to the camera's sight.

I focus. Refocus.
Your lines are true.
I hold my breath.
My breath holds you.

It's ready.
It's now.
It's …
CLICK!

You're history.

George Eastman left school when he was only fourteen. His father had died, and the family was poor. George had to support his mother and his two sisters.

As an office boy, George worked hard. When he grew up, he became a banker and worked even harder. Banking was tiring.

"I could use a break," said George, one day.

"You could use a hobby," said his mother.

George thought about hobbies. He liked pictures, but he couldn't paint. Maybe he could take pictures with a camera instead.

It was 1877. Cameras were the size of a microwave oven. And you needed lots of supplies to take a picture.

George was fond of making lists. He set out from home to get what he needed:

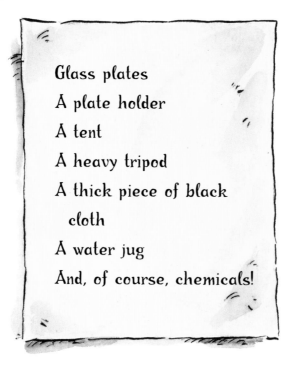

> Glass plates
> A plate holder
> A tent
> A heavy tripod
> A thick piece of black
>   cloth
> A water jug
> And, of course, chemicals!

George left the store loaded with gear. So far his new hobby was hard work!

George Eastman lived in Rochester, New York, where a stone bridge crossed the nearby river. It was the perfect spot for an outdoor shot.

One morning, George strapped the tent and the tripod to his back. He carried the camera, the plates, the plate holder, the black cloth, the water jug, and the chemicals. He felt like a packhorse! But he was ready to take a photograph.

On his way, the grocer stopped George. "Where are you going?" she asked.

"I'm off to take a photograph," replied George.

"This I've got to see," said the grocer.

Further down the road, the baker wanted to know where George and the grocer were going.

"George is off to take a photograph," replied the grocer.

"Wow!" said the baker. "This I've got to see."

The baker followed George and the grocer. And before you could say *scrambled eggs on toast*, the blacksmith, the cobbler, and half a dozen others were following George too!

At the stone bridge, George had a brain wave. "Bunch together, everyone," he shouted. "I'm going to take your photograph!"

"How exciting," said the grocer.

"You betcha," said the baker.

"I don't know anyone who can take a photograph," said the blacksmith.

"What's a photograph?" asked the cobbler.

George went into the tent to prepare the glass plate. He soaked it in the chemical tray. When the plate became cloudy, George raced to the camera. The plate could not dry out. If it did, George would have to start all over again.

The plate was soon in place. A black cloth covered George and his camera. Everyone stood still. George held his breath. *Snap!*

Back to the tent he went to develop the plate. George worked slowly and carefully. He could not drop the plate, or it would break. He could not spill the chemical, or it would eat holes in his clothes or burn his skin.

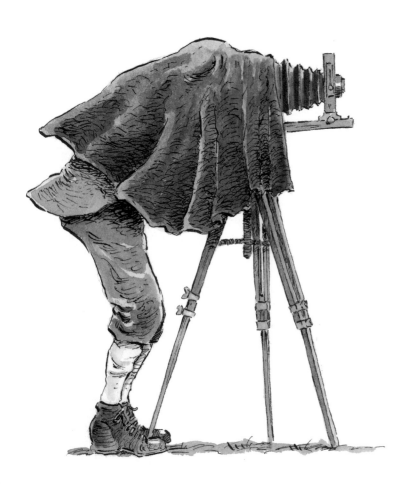

Time passed slowly. Everyone was bored.

"My shop is waiting for me," said the grocer.

"My horses are waiting for me," said the blacksmith.

The cobbler nodded. He had plenty of shoes with holes waiting for him.

Finally, the photograph was ready. George waved it in the air.

"Take a look everybody!" he shouted.

But George was on his own. Everybody had already gone back to town.

George Eastman loved his hobby.

"I wish everyone could take pictures," he said. "It's so much fun."

"Do something about it," suggested his mother.

Not many people could own a camera – they cost too much. A cheap one cost $25.00. It took weeks of hard work to make that kind of money!

"Dry plates would make picture-taking easier," said George. He wanted to make the camera as convenient as the pencil.

So, every day after work, George busied himself with his dry plates. He mixed the chemicals in his mother's kitchen. He baked the plates in his mother's oven. In the mornings, George's mother would find him asleep on the floor.

It took George three years to make a plate that worked. He tested it by taking a photograph of the house across the street.

"I did it!" shouted George.

"Happy news," said his mother. She wanted her kitchen back.

George's dry plates were a huge success. They were the best thing since swinging doors! Soon George made enough money to quit the bank. He opened his own dry-plate company in 1881.

It wasn't long before George thought dry plates were yesterday's news. He had another idea. Film! It took four years to make the first roll of film. It was a brand-new way to take pictures. *No fuss! No muss!*

"No more plates!" announced George.

"Wonderful," said his mother. She was getting tired of camera talk.

George's next idea was his best idea – a camera everyone could use!
It was small and light and came loaded with film.

George's new camera needed a name. He liked the sound of the
letter *K*. He put two of them in the name. KODAK sounded like the
click of a shutter.

George called his company the Eastman Kodak Company. He
even wrote his own ads – "You press the button. We do the rest."

The new camera caught on quickly. You could take a hundred photographs on just one roll of film! When the roll was done, you mailed it with the camera to the Eastman Kodak Company. Your pictures came back and so did your camera, loaded for more snapping!

George's camera was soon world-famous. But George wasn't finished with camera ideas. He wanted kids to get snap happy too. He called the new camera a Brownie. It cost only a dollar.

George Eastman's camera ideas made him rich. He built a fifty-room mansion in Rochester. His mother, who had always been poor, moved in with him. George wanted her to live in luxury.

George's mansion had all the modern conveniences. It had twenty-one telephones; a built-in vacuum cleaner; an elevator; and a large pipe organ. Every morning, an organist played the organ while George and his mother ate breakfast.

George was generous. He gave a lot of his money away. One of his first projects was a dental clinic in Rochester. Soon kids were having their teeth checked for a nickel.

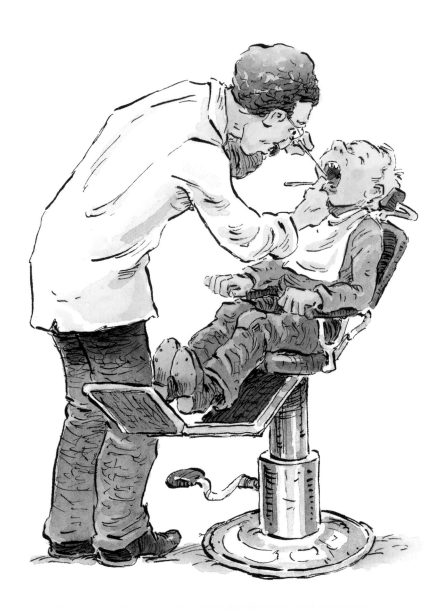

George took photographs all his life. You might call him a shutterbug. He was fond of the saying, "A picture is worth a thousand words."

When George traveled, he took pictures. When George stayed at home, he took pictures. He pointed his camera and framed the shot. Then he'd shout: "Say, cheese!" And people did.

Get Snap Happy!

The camera has come a long way since George Eastman's day. Today's digital cameras let you view your photos the moment you take them. You can download them onto your computer. You can e-mail them to friends, make a screen saver out of your favorite one, or print a copy to hang on your wall. All on the same day!

Pictures might be easy to snap, but they are better when you know what you're doing. Here are some tips to remember: *Frame your shot before you snap it.* You don't want a tree or pole sticking out of your friend's head! You don't want a lot of clutter in the picture either. *Move in close to get the best shot. Aim and shoot.* It's time to get snap happy!